INNOVATION PROVERBS
THE INNOVATOR'S ADVANTAGE

VOL. 1

Innovation Proverbs, Volume 1 By Dr. Evans Baiya
Copyright © 2023

Published by KDP

ISBN: 979-8386267773

This book does not contain legal advice. Author and publisher disclaim any and all warranties, liabilities, losses, costs, claims, demands, suits, or actions of any type or nature whatsoever arising from or in anyway related to this book, the use of this book, and/or any claims that a particular technique or device described in this book is legal or reasonable in any jurisdiction.

All rights reserved. No part of this book may be reproduced or transmitted in any form or by any means, electronic or mechanical, including photocopying, recording, or by any information storage and retrieval system, without written permission from the author, except for the inclusion of brief quotations in a review.

Praise for *Innovation Proverbs*, Volume 1
Early readers share insights on their favorite proverbs

STEVE MORRIS
Executive Advisor, Choice Works
Favorite Proverb, #48: It's not about perfection. It's about impact.

"In our interactions with clients, we often find this challenge with people who are high in compliance and steadiness and low in dominance and influence. They tend to be overly focused on perfection and avoiding mistakes. We offer the idea that 'Perfection is a thief.' People who are not willing to fail tend to fail to experiment as much as necessary to create velocity. Fail small, fast, and often to maximize the learning required to innovate. If you are not willing to fail, you will not maximize your innovation."

DR. JEREMY GRAVES
People Developer and Intergenerational Culture Strategist, Boise State University
Favorite Proverb, #17: One-person innovation teams are unsustainable.

"Collaboration is at the heart of what we do both within the university setting and with our business partners. This is a great reminder of the need to develop a collaborative mindset in all areas. Our business model within the university is built on working across boundaries and departments to create collaborative problem-solving teams. The best ideas come when multiple voices have a chance to share their perspectives. This allows for true collaboration and teams that will go beyond easy answers or one-person shows."

TIMOTHY WAEMA, PHD

Author, Professor, and Researcher of Information Systems, University of Nairobi

Favorite Proverb, #31: You don't innovate by chasing symptoms.

"We can abandon a potentially excellent idea because it failed, apparently because we tried to solve the symptoms and not the root cause."

TRISH CANDLER

Leadership and Team Coach

Favorite Proverb, #30: Always challenge the relevancy of what you're working on.

"So many times, we can get so stuck in the busyness of activities that we may lose sight of what else is going around us. When I ask myself the question, 'Is this still relevant?' it gives me permission to pause and reassess my strategy; it allows me to be more proactive and intentional with what I am working on."

TYLER ANDREW
President/CEO BBB Great West + Pacific
Favorite Proverb, #15: Great innovators ask great questions.

"This proverb resonates most with me because it's played an essential part of our innovation process. The question 'What problem are we trying to solve?' has been the foundation to our approach and has even led to a pivot of existing innovation projects. Constantly asking that question is so important!"

RICK MCPARTLIN
CEO, The Revenue Game, LLC
Favorite Proverb, #19: When you stop innovating, everyone can smell it.

"The only thing that assures (over 95%) a brand will survive is continually producing more profitable revenue. When revenue stops, the organization becomes insignificant and then goes out of business. This slide is a result of not having offers that buyers value enough to build enough volume and margin for profits to survive. The solution is to innovate new offers that the buyer values."

RYAN LISK
Executive Coach, Lisk Associates
Favorite Proverb, #8: Don't Be Slower Than Your Customer.

"This has several components to me. First, the tactical side: One of my annual business goals is to 'not be the cog in the wheel.' This means we don't want our clients to be waiting for us to complete projects. Second, the strategic side: We want to regularly ask our clients what they want, what today's people trends are, and how we can adapt to give them what they find value in."

PADRAIG BERRY
CEO, TTI Success Insights Ireland
Favorite Proverb, #1: Until action is taken, all ideas are worthless.

"In my experience, action raises one's self-esteem and performance, creating a virtuous cycle of success. It helps one's thinking—you get information/feedback, allowing you to clarify your thinking and modify your plans. It brings luck. When you take action, you see opportunities which allow you to make your own luck. It exposes obstacles which are stopping you from achieving your goals, allowing you to develop strategies to overcome them. It sharpens your animal instincts, which you can trust. The only reason you plan is so that you can take action. Plans in themselves are useless unless they are used as agents for action. It is what we do that defines who we are, not what we think, say, etc. One should regularly look at one's life and ask oneself the question, 'What have I done?' Then decide that the next time you ask yourself that question the answer will be more to your liking."

INTRODUCTION

Innovation isn't just about inventing new products. And innovators are not just inventors. If you are a leader working on improving anything, you are an innovator. It could be innovating your customer service flow, your sales processes, your new employee onboarding model, or your IT needs of the future. As systems struggle to evolve to new realities, innovators are needed more than ever.

Over the years, I've coached, consulted, and taught hundreds of innovators. In our conversations and planning sessions, I noticed a pattern of repeated sayings that applied to all innovators regardless of project or

Ron Price
President, TTI Success Insights

"Throughout my career, quotes have reminded me of what matters most. They pull me above the day-to-day busyness to call out my better self. Dr. Baiya has captured the essence of this experience in *Innovation Proverbs*! As I read through them, they re-focused my efforts on making each day count in creating value that makes a difference for others. With one proverb for each week of the year, they provide just the right rhythm to contemplate and act. As Evans wrote in the first proverb, 'Until action is taken, all ideas are worthless.' The concise nature of this book, and the potency of its insights, will make it a close companion for many years to come."

product. These sayings resonated with my clients and students, so I began to collect them. While brainstorming about these quotes with my team, I began to refer to them as "innovation proverbs." This long list of proverbs was pared down to the 52 you will find in this book: Volume I of *Innovation Proverbs*, with one proverb for each week of the year, although you may find your way through them more quickly. These quips have been inspired and informed by innovation, business, product design, and customer focus.

Of course, there are many, many books on innovation already in existence, so I didn't want to add another book to someone's unread pile. I wanted to create a book on innovation that no one had ever seen before. And I wanted to provide innovators with something they could consume and apply quickly. These proverbs are simple but concrete statements that are memorable and very applicable to the daily life of an innovator.

Most of these proverbs are moments of passion and insight that were captured by my clients and students. Many I wasn't aware of until they were repeated back to me by those clients! They shared with me that these proverbs were not only thought-provoking; they were also encouraging reminders and guidelines that maintained a timeless relevance.

Each proverb contains pithy usefulness combined with a deeper meaning. They allow room for introspection and interpretation according to the realities and perspectives of each reader. To assist with clarity, I have provided a brief explainer for each proverb, but the ultimate explanation is the experience that you have with them as you apply them!

I encourage you to not just skim these proverbs. Read them. Sit with them. Meditate on them. Let them take you to new places. Let them expand into your own sphere of knowledge. Blend them with your own hard-won proverbs and lessons.

These proverbs are meant to be shareable, evergreen conversation-starters. So please don't keep them to yourself! Share with your colleagues and peers, your boss, your investors. If you are a leader, I encourage you to incorporate these proverbs into the innovation processes and trainings within your organization. You will find that they apply to every area of your business. As such, spread them like seeds and watch new innovations and stories sprout!

Keep Innovating!
Evans Baiya

UNTIL ACTION IS TAKEN, ALL IDEAS ARE WORTHLESS.

— DR. EVANS BAIYA

IA | THEINNOVATORSADVANTAGE.COM

All ideas start with the same value: zero! This is why the value of an idea is directly proportional to the action taken to execute it. The next time you have an idea, sit with it. Think deeper, imagine wider, discuss it with others, and then ask, "What action can I take to make this idea real?" Then do it! With thoughtful action, the idea starts to become both viable and valuable.

HONOR THE *COURAGE* IT TAKES TO SHARE A NEW IDEA.

—DR. EVANS BAIYA

 THEINNOVATORSADVANTAGE.COM

Ideas are the "children" of our brains. It takes energy, sweat, or stress to come up with ideas. And even more to share an idea! That's because sharing an idea means you are exposing your "child" to the atmosphere, to the world, to the opinions of others. So next time someone voices their idea, listen, acknowledge—and judge the quality and content of their idea later.

INNOVATION PROVERBS

THE PRIMARY INDICATOR OF AN INNOVATIVE CULTURE IS *THE FREE EXCHANGE OF IDEAS.*

— DR. EVANS BAIYA

IA | THEINNOVATORSADVANTAGE.COM

Economic value is determined by the value of the currency. The same is true with the innovation economy, where the currency is ideas. The more ideas you have, the higher the likelihood of being successful in this economy—the higher the likelihood of creating an innovative culture. The stronger the culture of innovation, the stronger the economic potential.

IF YOU WANT TO SOLVE A *BIG PROBLEM,* GATHER AS MANY IDEAS AS POSSIBLE.

— DR. EVANS BAIYA

 THEINNOVATORSADVANTAGE.COM

Nature teaches that it takes as many seeds as possible to sustain life. The same is true with ideas. A single idea is just a seed. The more complex a problem, the more ideas are needed. To truly sustain innovation and solve big problems, plant as many seeds as possible. The next time you have an idea you love, think of how you can add more ideas, and expand it so it can grow.

BLENDING TOGETHER MULTIPLE IDEAS EXPONENTIALLY *MULTIPLIES THE VALUE OF EACH IDEA.*

— DR. EVANS BAIYA

 theinnovatorsadvantage.com

An idea plus another idea doesn't equal two ideas. It equals multiple ideas. This is an important concept when you are trying to solve a significant problem or create a new solution. Consider a cheeseburger. It's a combination of ideas—the meat, the cheese, the bun, the condiments—that all work just fine by themselves, but once you bring them together you create a new product and the value increases exponentially.

BOLD IDEAS SPARK *PROGRESS.* TIMID IDEAS *SUCK.*

— DR. EVANS BAIYA

 THEINNOVATORSADVANTAGE.COM

Protecting the status quo or stating the obvious is not innovation. In fact, they are the opposite of innovation. They don't challenge systems. They don't inspire change. They only produce boredom and lifelessness. Bold ideas make you feel alive! They make you think more deeply. They stir emotions, inspire creativity, stoke imagination—and ultimately bring you to bigger and better ideas.

INNOVATION PROVERBS

ALWAYS BE THINKING ABOUT WHO COULD BE YOUR NEXT *CUSTOMER.*

—DR. EVANS BAIYA

IA | theinnovatorsadvantage.com

According to Peter Drucker, the purpose of business is to create a customer. That mandate is truer than ever. To continue to innovate, we must consistently and constantly be looking for new customers. Ideators look for ideas, but innovators look for new customers in both expected and unexpected places. Your next customer will be found in solving a problem they are having or bringing awareness to a solution they don't even know they need.

INNOVATION PROVERBS

DON'T BE *SLOWER* THAN YOUR CUSTOMER.

— DR. EVANS BAIYA

 THEINNOVATORSADVANTAGE.COM

The life of a customer is always changing. Because of this, customers are always looking for new solutions and better value. It is important to know what your customers are looking for at any given time. If you cannot move at the same speed or faster than your customer, you will be left behind and your customers will simply forget about you. This is highly preventable! Agility and the ability to anticipate and respond to their needs is the secret to sustained innovation.

💡 INNOVATION PROVERBS

IT'S NOT INNOVATION UNTIL *THE CUSTOMER CARES.*

— DR. EVANS BAIYA

 theinnovatorsadvantage.com

Research, experiments, and data points are important parts of the innovation process. But the customer doesn't care. They want to know how they can use your product to get their job done, not what you did to create it. Instead, focus on the job to be done for the customer. Do not overwhelm your customer with experiments and data. And make it as easy as possible for your customers to do their own experiments with your product!

INNOVATION PROVERBS

IF YOU SOLVE YOUR CUSTOMERS' *PROBLEMS,* THEY WILL SOLVE *YOURS.*

— DR. EVANS BAIYA

 THEINNOVATORSADVANTAGE.COM

*T*here is a symbiotic relationship between your revenue and your relationship with your customers. If you want to solve your problem of generating revenue, you need to focus first on solving their problem. This means talking less about your product and focusing on demonstrating how it can be useful and helpful in solving their problem. It is not your specs that convince customers to buy. It is your relating to them and solving the problem that inspires them to buy. And inspiring them to buy is how they solve your revenue issues!

INNOVATION PROVERBS

A PURCHASE IS THE ULTIMATE VALIDATION OF INNOVATION.

— DR. EVANS BAIYA

IA | THEINNOVATORSADVANTAGE.COM

11

Imagine coming up with a five-wheeled car that is faster and more stable than a four-wheeled car. This has been tried before. So why don't we have more five-wheeled cars on our roads? The truth is that it is only a cool feature. The market has spoken and the majority of drivers have decided having a fifth wheel is not necessary. Innovation is the same. The idea with the most features and adornments doesn't validate innovation. Validation comes from the solution that creates the greatest value for the customers who buy it.

INNOVATION PROVERBS

STOP OFFERING CUSTOMERS WHAT THEY DON'T NEED.

— DR. EVANS BAIYA

 THEINNOVATORSADVANTAGE.COM

For many customers, time and attention are their most valuable assets. The surest way to lose a customer is to offer them what they don't need. When you offer your customers something they don't need, it actually creates confusion and even frustration with your brand. It breeds distrust. Customers become less inclined to listen to you because they think you don't listen to them or understand them. When you understand the customer's problem, only then is your product worthy of their time and attention.

OVER-EXPLAINING CREATES *FRICTION.*

— DR. EVANS BAIYA

IA | theinnovatorsadvantage.com

A strong offer is a 10-second message or less. Make your offer simple and clear. "We provide X so you can do Y." "We make X so you can be Y." When the job to be done is clear, the value is clear to the customer. Get to this place as quickly as possible! Don't waste their time by over-explaining your features. The features don't sell a product or service; it's the clarity of the solution that causes customers to buy. Discipline yourself to focus on what is differentiating and most impactful for the customer.

INNOVATION PROVERBS

HOW MUCH YOU LOVE YOUR CUSTOMERS *RIGHT NOW* REVEALS YOUR *FUTURE.*

— DR. EVANS BAIYA

THEINNOVATORSADVANTAGE.COM

Customers dictate the past, the present, and the future of your business. Tell me about your customers in the past, and I'll tell you what kind of customers you have now. Tell me how you're expanding your customer base, and I'll tell you what your future customers are like. Focus your energy on loving your customers right now, and they will reward you by being there in the future to purchase from you. There is no substitute for love; it's the customer's language.

INNOVATION PROVERBS

GREAT INNOVATORS ASK GREAT QUESTIONS.

— DR. EVANS BAIYA

IA | THEINNOVATORSADVANTAGE.COM

Asking great questions is a hallmark of a great innovator. The most important question an innovator can ask is, "What problem or what opportunity can I solve?" This is only the beginning of the many questions that great innovators must ask themselves before they commit to developing their innovation. Asking great questions is a skill every innovator must develop. Once you have this skill, you will get better answers—guaranteeing you a better shot at creating the right solution for the right customer.

INNOVATION PROVERBS

DECISION-MAKING COMES BEFORE *PROBLEM-SOLVING.*

—DR. EVANS BAIYA

IA THEINNOVATORSADVANTAGE.COM

Newton's Second Law of Motion says that every action produces a reaction. This means that every problem calls for some type of solution. However, when you focus on problem-solving first, you might be tempted to develop the solution first, even before it is the right solution for the right context. The more urgent decision is to determine if the problem is worth solving. All other decisions originate from this decision.

INNOVATION PROVERBS

ONE-PERSON INNOVATION TEAMS ARE *UNSUSTAINABLE.*

—DR. EVANS BAIYA

IA theinnovatorsadvantage.com

Have you ever seen a one-person band? It's entertaining for a moment, but not that great. If you really want to enjoy a concert, it takes a number of expert players. The same is true with innovation. You need a well-rounded team to execute innovation. When someone thinks they are so brilliant that they can solve all problems and come up with all the good ideas alone, it means they don't understand that true innovation is a team effort. If you want to solve significant problems or come up with big ideas, you need others—their input, ideas, expertise, and hard work.

INNOVATION PROVERBS

DO NOT LET DOUBTING YOUR IDEAS BECOME DOUBTING YOURSELF.

— DR. EVANS BAIYA

IA | THEINNOVATORSADVANTAGE.COM

Few people start out as amazing ideators. Ideation is a skill, and we all have the potential for developing this skill. You may feel that you don't come up with great ideas. Perhaps it's because you compare yourself with others. Just remember, you won't get your best idea the first time. But keep learning the skill of ideation. The more you practice ideation, the more your confidence will grow—and soon your ability to contribute more and better ideas will also grow.

INNOVATION PROVERBS

WHEN YOU STOP INNOVATING, EVERYONE CAN SMELL IT.

—DR. EVANS BAIYA

IA | THEINNOVATORSADVANTAGE.COM

You smell it when a brand begins to drift. Nothing produces an aroma like stagnation or irrelevance. This comes from your solution being surpassed by superior technology, the arrogance that you don't need to innovate, and/or a culture of complacency. This can be prevented! Listen to the marketplace, create a culture of innovation, and ask your customers what their next need is.

INNOVATION PROVERBS

AN INNOVATOR'S FIRST JOB IS TO *THINK.*

—DR. EVANS BAIYA

IA | THEINNOVATORSADVANTAGE.COM

Innovation starts with and is propelled by ideas. Ideas come through thinking. Innovators need to make thinking an essential priority and activity, one that is far more important than busywork. There are many ways to think—conceptual thinking, futuristic thinking, problem-solving, connecting ideas, substituting, and more. The amount of time you spend on thinking will be reflected in the value of your innovations.

INNOVATION PROVERBS

CRITICAL THINKING IS ALWAYS AN ACT OF COURAGE.

— DR. EVANS BAIYA

IA THEINNOVATORSADVANTAGE.COM

Henry Ford famously said, "You can have any color you want as long as it is black." GM challenged that thinking. They listened to the marketplace and discovered that people wanted to stand out by having different colors, shapes, and sizes of cars. GM started selling colored vehicles and changed the industry forever. This happens often in business. Somebody identifies a revenue stream, and everybody wants to copy the first mover who had success. Soon everyone is running the same ads and speaking the same language and customers are bored to death. Customers quickly move onto something that makes them different from other customers. Think differently and add some color to your customers. Don't copy; innovate!

INNOVATION PROVERBS

AGILITY IS A *MINDSET* BEFORE IT IS A *TECHNIQUE.*

— DR. EVANS BAIYA

IA theinnovatorsadvantage.com

Agility is often thought of as a production methodology. But before agility can be a process or a technique, it has to be a principle—a mindset that says you are flexible and willing to learn at the speed of feedback and data, that you collaborate with the right people and work iteratively. Without an agile mindset, agility is just another methodology.

INNOVATION PROVERBS

INNOVATORS EMBRACE TENSION.

— DR. EVANS BAIYA

IA | THEINNOVATORSADVANTAGE.COM

There's only one guarantee in innovation: You will not get what you want the first time. This creates a consistent tension between the envisioned outcome, the work that needs to be done, and the possibility that the outcomes will be different. You have to deal with the reality that even the best of ideas may not see the light of day, and that is part of the risk of being an innovator. Embrace that tension and innovate anyway!

INNOVATION PROVERBS

INNOVATORS ALWAYS PRODUCE *VALUE.*

— DR. EVANS BAIYA

IA | theinnovatorsadvantage.com

The essence of innovation is to improve the current state and the possibility of a better future. If your activities don't improve the current context or create a brighter future, you are not innovating. You are not adding value to anyone, including yourself. To be regarded as an innovator, it's not a matter of scope and size. It's a matter of whether what you come up with is valuable, useful, and helpful.

INNOVATION PROVERBS

Speed of Learning is the New Unfair Advantage.

— Dr. Evans Baiya

IA | theinnovatorsadvantage.com

Nothing will create value and excitement for the future more than an organization focused on learning. Seek, analyze, and create insights around trends specific to your customers so that you can provide solutions, even before your customers think of them. When you increase the speed of learning, you increase the value of your brand. If you want to beat your competition, be a futurist in the eyes of your customers.

INNOVATION PROVERBS

DON'T SELL THE OBVIOUS.

—DR. EVANS BAIYA

IA theinnovatorsadvantage.com

When the room is cold, the obvious is to turn on the heater. That is the basic logic, right? But do you actually want warmth, or do you want to feel comfortable? The problem with selling the obvious is that so is everyone else! By providing a solution for the actual needs of the customer, your solution is always of higher value. Sell "comfort," not "warmth."

INNOVATION PROVERBS

INNOVATORS ARE CONSTANLY *DISRUPTING THEMSELVES.*

— DR. EVANS BAIYA

IA | THEINNOVATORSADVANTAGE.COM

Innovators never blame changes in the market, current events, or conditions. They don't fear these factors because they are constantly disrupting their own business models, processes, and products. Because they embrace a growth mindset, they are more prepared to take advantage of volatility and uncertainty. Innovators know that no matter what happens there will always be new opportunities to create value.

INNOVATION PROVERBS

UNIQUENESS IS *TEMPORARY.*

— DR. EVANS BAIYA

theinnovatorsadvantage.com

What is the expiration date of your uniqueness? Every innovation has an expiration date. If what makes you unique is within striking distance of your competition, then one adjustment by them can make you instantly irrelevant. Innovators are always two or three steps ahead—looking for ways to create a competitive advantage so when their competitors try to copy them, their uniqueness and market position have already evolved.

INNOVATION PROVERBS

YOU ARE AN IDEA FARM.
YOU ARE ALWAYS CAPABLE OF GENERATING NEW IDEAS.

—DR. EVANS BAIYA

IA | THEINNOVATORSADVANTAGE.COM

29

As long as your brain is alive, you are blessed with the ability to be creative. Your brain is endlessly capable of coming up with ideas. However, creativity is a learned skill and practice. You have to train your brain to become a productive idea farm. You become an idea farm by investing in what is already within you, nurturing it, guarding it, and growing it.

INNOVATION PROVERBS

ALWAYS CHALLENGE THE *RELEVANCY* OF WHAT YOU'RE WORKING ON.

— DR. EVANS BAIYA

theinnovatorsadvantage.com

"Is this still relevant?" This is the question that challenges the agility of your strategy. If you ignore this question, you either have dumb luck or you are out of business! The world can change in an instant. This means that relevancy changes too. Your strategy and ensuing ideas need to be flexible enough to not only adjust to these changes but to take advantage of them. Always find the edge of what you are working on.

INNOVATION PROVERBS

YOU DON'T INNOVATE BY CHASING SYMPTOMS.

—DR. EVANS BAIYA

IA | THEINNOVATORSADVANTAGE.COM

What you see on the surface is most likely not the cause of the problem that needs to be solved. There's always an underlying cause. Failing at innovation isn't the root cause. It's the result of focusing on the symptoms. Innovation didn't fail. Analysis of the actual problem failed. Employee turnover or being beaten by the competition are symptoms of a deeper problem—likely a lack of innovation!

💡 **INNOVATION PROVERBS**

> # AS LONG AS YOU ARE CREATING THE RIGHT VALUE, *YOU ARE INNOVATING.*
>
> —DR. EVANS BAIYA

theinnovatorsadvantage.com

Innovators don't get rewarded by identifying a problem and creating a solution. Everyone is already doing that! Innovators get rewarded for creating and delivering the right value for the right customer at the right time. If you can't add the right value, it doesn't matter how cool your solution is.

INNOVATION PROVERBS

DATA IS A TOOL FOR *INNOVATING,* NOT THE INNOVATION ITSELF.

—DR. EVANS BAIYA

IA THEINNOVATORSADVANTAGE.COM

Every activity in business creates data. If it was about the presence of data, we would all be richly innovative. It is how we start using the data that matters. The presence of data without innovation is like being a poor farmer who owns land that doesn't produce rich crops, yet underneath the soil lies gold. Land is data, using the land is innovation.

INNOVATION PROVERBS

WITHOUT CUSTOMER VALIDATION, THERE IS NO INNOVATION.

—DR. EVANS BAIYA

THEINNOVATORSADVANTAGE.COM

The beauty of innovation is that there is always a moment of truth: Does the customer think your product or service is worth buying or not? When we've poured so much into innovation, we don't want to hear that the customer won't buy. However, without validation, you have no credibility. Without that moment of truth, you have no mandate for claiming yourself to be an innovator. Without validation, you are just someone claiming they won a game they never actually played.

INNOVATION PROVERBS

THE CUSTOMER'S JOB IS TO JUDGE YOU. EMBRACE THAT.

—DR. EVANS BAIYA

THEINNOVATORSADVANTAGE.COM

Your customers hold the power to decide how much attention they give you, if they will buy from you, and if they will talk about you. Your customers are independent thinkers with a separate decision-making authority. They don't think what you tell them. So of course they are judging you. Let them judge you! It will make you better!

INNOVATION PROVERBS

ASK FOR FEEBACK.
SOME OF IT IS HELPFUL.

—DR. EVANS BAIYA

IA | THEINNOVATORSADVANTAGE.COM

Hopefully, when you expose your product to the customer, they will respond positively. But you must also expect that the customer may say it is not useful to them. Unexpected negative feedback reveals blind spots and flaws—and gives you the opportunity to learn and create value. Even if you disagree with their feedback, you will have added value to yourself and your organization through learning, experimentation, humility, and receptiveness.

INNOVATION PROVERBS

SOMETIMES LEAVING THE PROBLEM UNSOLVED IS THE SOLUTION.

— DR. EVANS BAIYA

theinnovatorsadvantage.com

Not every problem is worth solving. Especially if you are just reacting to the whims of the customer or a competitor's strategy. Sit and observe the problem for a while. Study it and understand it. If it becomes clear that there is a problem to solve, then by all means develop a solution! But you will find that most "problems" are just distractions. Stay focused!

INNOVATION PROVERBS

> **IF YOU ARE GOING TO BE A SOLUTION LOOKING FOR A PROBLEM, FIRST EDUCATE THE MARKET ON THE PROBLEM.**
>
> — DR. EVANS BAIYA

THEINNOVATORSADVANTAGE.COM

A lot of businesses start out this way: They come up with a solution, then go looking for a problem to solve with it. This is often discouraged, but here is a different take: If you can educate the market on the problem, then you can create demand for your product. In many ways, that's what innovation is—giving people what they didn't even know they needed.

INNOVATION PROVERBS

TOO MANY OPINIONS KILL *CLARITY.*

— DR. EVANS BAIYA

IA theinnovatorsadvantage.com

This is a challenge for many companies. They want to provide multiple options to customers. They create their version of The Cheesecake Factory menu. All this does is contribute to decision fatigue. Give your customers a break by making options simple and clear. They will reward you by buying faster and paying more because they know exactly what to expect.

INNOVATION PROVERBS

SOME PROBLEMS AREN'T PROBLEMS.
THEY ARE IDEAS.

— DR. EVANS BAIYA

IA | THEINNOVATORSADVANTAGE.COM

Can you express a problem in the form of an idea? If so, you can unlock the creative part of your brain and come up with technological, functional, and even social solutions to the problem. An example: "I am feeling cold" is a problem. Instead, phrase that as, "How can I feel warmer?" Now you aren't complaining, you're creating!

INNOVATION PROVERBS

FORGETTING TO EXPERIMENT IS *STUPID.*

—DR. EVANS BAIYA

IA | THEINNOVATORSADVANTAGE.COM

Experiments help us make better decisions and reduce risk. If you are not running experiments, you are guessing. And guessing is, well, stupid. Sometimes not experimenting is forgetfulness. You are excited to get your idea to market! But taking time to experiment ensures a greater chance of success. Sometimes not experimenting is arrogance. But no product is perfect the first time. Don't be stupid, be humble.

INNOVATION PROVERBS

THE VOLUME OF EXPERIMENTATION IS IN DIRECT PROPORTION TO THE LEVEL OF *INNOVATION*.

— DR. EVANS BAIYA

IA THEINNOVATORSADVANTAGE.COM

42

Complex products require a complex approach to experimentation. In order to detangle complexity, you need to create a systematic approach to examining and testing the various components. Many small improvements through experimentation lead to a much better product in the end. Consider an apple pie. You don't just throw everything together, put it in the oven, and hope it turns out OK. Baking it and tasting it is experimentation. Now, you want to improve your apple pie. In order to do this, you must think about improvements at each step in the recipe.

INNOVATION PROVERBS

EVERY TIME YOU SOLVE A *PROBLEM,* YOU CREATE *VALUE.*

— DR. EVANS BAIYA

IA | THEINNOVATORSADVANTAGE.COM

43

Look for problems, solve them, and someone will pay you for them. The complexities of modern business and life result in a myriad of problems that provide you the opportunity to create different kinds of value. There are five types of value: social, economic, convenience, function, and design. In order for your idea to be a solution, it must provide at least one of these five types of value. So what value are you creating?

INNOVATION PROVERBS

> **THE FUTURE IS DETERMINED BY *INNOVATORS*. EVERYONE ELSE IS AN *ADOPTER*.**
>
> —DR. EVANS BAIYA

theinnovatorsadvantage.com

*I*nnovators lead. Everybody else follows. Innovators set the pace for the future. Throughout history, we have witnessed those who invented world-changing innovations that dictated what happened next. When Guttenberg invented the printing press, it birthed a new industry and changed life as we know it. That invention ultimately inspired electronic communication and then the internet and the digital age. All because of one great innovator who led the way. In your context, how are you leading?

INNOVATION PROVERBS

BLESSED ARE THOSE WHO KNOW HOW TO SOLVE PROBLEMS, FOR THEY SHALL *NEVER* RUN OUT OF WORK.

—DR. EVANS BAIYA

IA THEINNOVATORSADVANTAGE.COM

The very essence of business is to solve problems. And there are always endless problems to solve! As such, those who are skilled at solving problems are always in demand. They make the world better, and everybody wants to work with them. Great problem-solvers don't see obstacles as a stopping point. They don't think of the limitations; they have a growth mindset. As such, they are always in demand—and can often set their own value.

INNOVATION PROVERBS

IF YOU ARE NOT CHANGING *DIRECTION*, YOU ARE NOT *PIVOTING.*

— DR. EVANS BAIYA

theinnovatorsadvantage.com

A true pivot is a change of direction based on new information. Many organizations say they are pivoting, but they haven't actually changed directions. They say they are pivoting but are not ready to change their minds, their systems, or their processes. So, they talk and talk about pivoting but never actually do it.

INNOVATION PROVERBS

> "A LACK OF UNDERSTANDING OF THE TRAJECTORY OF A SOLUTION CAN *KILL* A BUSINESS."
>
> — DR. EVANS BAIYA
>
> theinnovatorsadvantage.com

47

What happens when you have the right product but a poor understanding of the potential of a market? That is the story of Kodak. They invented digital photography. However, they miscalculated its value and where the customer was going. As such, they lost momentum because they were not prepared, and eventually competition took advantage. You can be the first to invent a product, but if you are not the first to market, then this lack of understanding of the trajectory of a product can kill momentum—and your business.

INNOVATION PROVERBS

IT'S NOT ABOUT PERFECTION.
IT'S ABOUT *IMPACT.*

— DR. EVANS BAIYA

theinnovatorsadvantage.com

We have so many examples of inventors losing opportunities because they were trying to make their product perfect. A product that's 70% ready and then launched to market will produce more revenue than a product that's 100% ready but missed the launch window. Impact is the ultimate reward for innovation, but it requires velocity. And perfection is the enemy of velocity. So get impact first; get "perfect" later.

INNOVATION PROVERBS

ALMOST ANY REVENUE CRISIS CAN BE SOLVED BY *DOUBLING DOWN* ON CUSTOMER FOCUS.

— DR. EVANS BAIYA

IA THEINNOVATORSADVANTAGE.COM

Revenue desperation is a major enemy of successful innovation. It often produces short-sighted and delusional tactics, which inevitably leads to increased stress and decreased innovation. Even worse, it causes you to take your eye off the main focus: the customer! The customer doesn't care if you are profitable or not. What is paramount to them is that you actually solve their problems. No matter the revenue situation, always keep the customer first and revenue second. If you align these well, then you will be profitable.

INNOVATION PROVERBS

FIRE YOURSELF. THEN REHIRE YOURSELF FOR THE *FUTURE* YOU WANT.

— DR. EVANS BAIYA

IA | theinnovatorsadvantage.com

The biggest challenge with stagnant organizations is that leaders can lack perspective. They live under the pressure of the current moment. They rarely think about the future—especially optimistically. Getting a fresh perspective often requires you to do something bold. Sometimes it takes being outside your company to experience a different world, to be able to think differently about how to add value and attract new customers. So try quitting your organization. Go somewhere else to learn and change perspective, and then come back. Or if you can, fire yourself by taking a long sabbatical, then return and re-engage with new energy.

INNOVATION PROVERBS

UNIQUE PROBLEMS NEVER CREATE SCALABLE SOLUTIONS.

— DR. EVANS BAIYA

IA THEINNOVATORSADVANTAGE.COM

51

A common mistake is hearing about a problem and then rushing to develop a solution. Sometimes the problems are based on a specific context. Solving an anomaly or one-time problem is a poor use of resources. Next time your customer asks you to solve a problem, you first need to understand and verify if it is a broader issue. This means listening carefully to your customer, then interviewing as many different customers as possible to determine if it is a problem you should actually solve.

INNOVATION PROVERBS

BE *BRUTALLY HONEST* ABOUT THE *EXCUSES* THAT ARE *LIMITING* INNOVATION.

— DR. EVANS BAIYA

IA THEINNOVATORSADVANTAGE.COM

It is important to admit that you are not innovating, but it is inexcusable and outright dangerous for you to be ignorant about why you are not innovating. Is it due to a lack of talent, funds, or future perspective? Status quo? Being clear about why you are not innovating may eventually help you come up with a way to start innovating. If you are not searching for answers, you are just burying your head in the sand, hoping the tide never comes in. In other words, you are dying a slow guaranteed death.

INNOVATION PROVERBS

AFTERWORD

"Helloooooooo, Justin! So good to see you!" It had been awhile since I'd heard the melodic cheerfulness of Evans' voice. Since meeting in 2012, I've been a witness to Evans' growth and trajectory as a truly original thought leader. I've always admired his brilliant and nimble mind and his enormous heart for others.

"I would love your help on a project," he said. Evans went on to tell me about these proverbs that he'd collected over the years. Or more accurately, proverbs that he shared with his many clients and students and they collected for him. My role was to help refine and sharpen each of the proverbs. To do this, we created a framework:

- Original—none of them could be perceived as being borrowed re-hashings or re-purposings of other people's quotes.

- Insightful—they had to make the reader pause and think, then spark a moment of revelation.

- Provocative—they had to challenge the reader's biases assumptions. We wanted each to cause the reader to say, "I never thought about it that way before!"

- Conversational—they had to be pithy and intellectually stimulating without becoming too esoteric or academic.

Finally, the proverbs needed to remain in Evans' voice—that unique blend of brilliance, joyfulness, and infinite possibility.

I felt like I had been given a box of 52 diamonds. As I polished, cut, and defined each of them, I began to notice how quickly my mind adopted them. They started to pop into my conversations at home and with friends and clients. I found myself at least once a day saying some variation of: "That reminds me of a proverb from my friend Evans."

One of my deepest intentions is to inspire more contemplativeness in people—especially in the business world. Americans, in particular, are intensely extrinsic with a lot of inner worry and angst but not much sitting quietly and thinking about their inner world. I'm also drawn to originality. There are many "karaoke singers" who call themselves thought leaders but are actually regurgitating other people's ideas—and often claiming these ideas for their own. As author and speaker Rob Bell says, "Quote yourself!" To quote yourself requires a deep and insistent inner curiosity combined with a risk-taking, bias-busting outer curiosity. It requires the humility to be receptive to downloads from the Universe while having the boldness and courage to share them with the world. Being an original means knowing yourself. It means having a spirit of "namaste" that sees the priceless worth in yourself and others.

Evans is all of these.

The world needs more innovators. Not just people inventing new products but innovators creating the tools and methodologies that advance humanity and contribute to much-needed and urgent systemic change. So please use these proverbs in your life. Let each of them become a source of inner inspiration and an igniter of deeper conversations. May their timeless wisdom activate the timeless wisdom contained within you.

> Justin Foster
> @ **fosterthinking**
> **Austin, Texas**

More Advanced Reader Praise
Innovation Proverbs, Volume 1

EMMANUEL LAI
Co-founder, Heaven's Pantry
Favorite Proverb, #18: Do not let doubting your ideas become doubting yourself.

"Intelligent people, due to possessing a sense of natural skepticism, have a tendency to doubt their own ideas. Those who are hypercritical of their ideas should recognize that it is not a sign of inadequacy, but rather a sign of intelligence. Understanding that their minds are like furnaces forging gold, such a person should sleep well, knowing that the fire which burns within will melt away the flaws and impurities of their original idea. Once this process of purification is completed, they will have a marked advantage in the phase of execution compared to their counterparts who do not doubt themselves."

MAUREEN ENNIS
Leadership Advisor, Thrive
Favorite Proverb, #2: Honor the courage it takes to share a new idea.

"In my experience working with organizations of all sizes, I find this is one of their biggest challenges. I believe over the last few decades we have ingrained practice and efficiency to such a level that there is a fear of taking chances to even speak up with good ideas. Certainly, psychological safety goes right to this point. It does all start with honoring people who have the courage to speak up and make themselves vulnerable by sharing a good idea."

ANURADHA KHODA, PHD
eLearning Strategy Advisor
Favorite Proverb, #32: As long as you are creating the right value, you are innovating.

"I particularly like this one. Innovation is not about a novelty but about packaging the right product or service in the most appropriate way at the right time, so the user feels like the given solution never existed before."

DALTON COX
Organizational Development Specialist, Bovo-Tighe
Favorite Proverb, #5: Blending together multiple ideas exponentially multiplies the value of each idea.

"I really liked the cheeseburger analogy. It got me thinking… I also really enjoy sushi, which has very few ingredients, yet is still delicious. Reminding me that blending ideas together isn't always about adding things; it can also be about refinement. Ideas and feedback can highlight what to focus on and what to take away—not just make things more complex."

JUDY KNIGHT
Executive Coach, Thumbprint Coaching, Inc.
Favorite Proverb, #9: It's not innovation until the customer cares.

"It puts in perspective that we are innovating not just for the fun and thrill of it. It needs to meet a customer need. This is a bottom-line piece of guidance for me."

MARIE-JOSEE HALEY
Business Advisor, Propriétaire
Favorite Proverb, #45: Blessed are those who know how to solve problems, for they shall never run out of work.

"This proverb was refreshing, and I could recognize myself in it. I love to solve problems; in fact, they are not problems to me, they are opportunities to get better. It had a positive and reassuring impact this morning. Let's make the world better."

SAM FIFE
Innovation Director, BBB Great West + Pacific
Favorite Proverb, #50: Fire yourself. Then rehire yourself for the future you want.

"When I first heard this proverb from Evans three years ago, it struck me as such an odd suggestion. The last thing I want to be is fired. But as I worked through it, I was able to release many of the 'untouchable' pieces of my role and my team's work and see it through new eyes. In the time since, we have redesigned that business function from the ground up to add tangible value to customers through a service that was little more than a resource drain at the time."

TANJA YARDLEY
Leadership and Innovation Coach, HealthTech Connex Inc.
Favorite Proverb, #27: Innovators are constantly disrupting themselves.

"This is such a key aspect of innovation... complacency is the enemy. We must be willing to burn things down and rise from the ashes once in a while."

DALTON COX
Organizational Development Specialist, Bovo-Tighe

"Not only are they great to meditate on, but I also especially like the conversational nature of them. They'd be great to discuss with others throughout the week. These proverbs also do a great job of capturing the Evans essence/voice—that unique blend of brilliance, joyfulness, and infinite possibilities."

MARIE-JOSEE HALEY
Business Advisor, Propriétaire

"I hope you will also take the time to read one proverb a week, in order or randomly and listen to how it resonates with you, how it influences you, how it inspires you to act differently. Enjoy and be an innovator!"

DR. FRANCIS EBERLE
Leadership & Strategy Advisor, Price Associates

"Evans has created a collection of innovation insights that at first glance might seem simple. Yet with reflection, it soon becomes apparent they are powerful reminders of our humanness and our need to focus when innovating. Innovation has many dimensions, and they are wonderfully captured here with clarity and a path forward."

About Evans Baiya

Evans Baiya is a scientist, consultant, author, and speaker. He has tackled innovation, strategy, and technology from all angles—as a researcher, technologist, and executive in multiple start-ups, global leader of research and development efforts in multiple countries, intellectual property portfolio manager at a global corporation, and policy advisor on research and commercialization.

He works with organizations on strategy and planning, R&D and innovation programs, technology transfer, commercialization, digital transformation, data and analytics, and cybersecurity. He is the co-author of *The Innovator's Advantage: Revealing the Hidden Connection Between People and Process* (2017) and *Optimizing Strategy for Results: A Structured Approach to Make Your Business Come Alive* (2022).

Made in the USA
Columbia, SC
22 June 2023